Contents

Rigby®

A Harcourt Achieve Imprint

www.Rigby.com
1-800-531-5015

1 The Ride of Your Life

Your heart pounding with excitement, you slide into the seat of the roller coaster and lower the safety bar over your body. A few moments later, the coaster shakes to life and roars down the track. Bravely you face what is coming next. As the coaster slowly climbs up a steep hill, you clutch the safety bar tightly.

"Clank—clank—clank!" you hear. As the first car peeks over the top of the hill, it seems to hesitate for a moment until . . .

Down the roller coaster plunges, straight toward the ground! People around you scream, but you hold your breath, feeling like your stomach has jumped up into your throat. Up and down your car twirls and turns, shudders and dives, climbs and dips. Finally the roller coaster glides back into the station. The instant it stops, you jump out of the car and run back to the line so you can ride again!

Some people scream as the roller coaster glides around the track while others let go of the car and put their arms in the air!

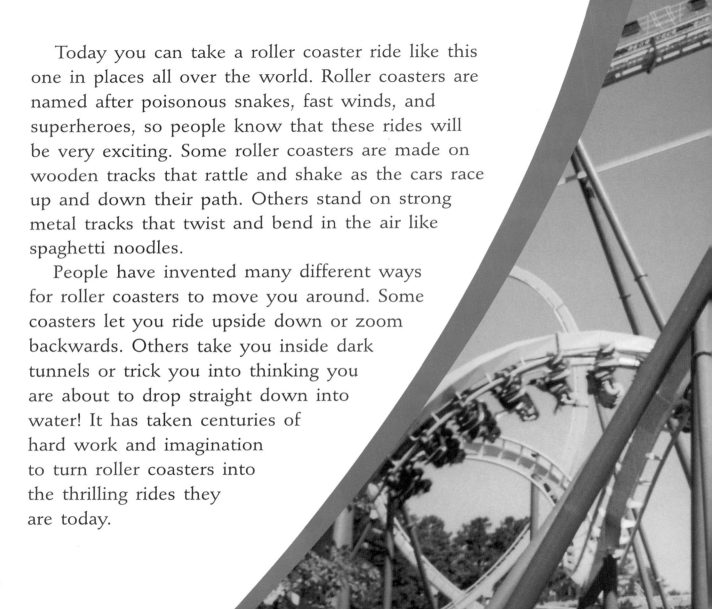

Today you can take a roller coaster ride like this one in places all over the world. Roller coasters are named after poisonous snakes, fast winds, and superheroes, so people know that these rides will be very exciting. Some roller coasters are made on wooden tracks that rattle and shake as the cars race up and down their path. Others stand on strong metal tracks that twist and bend in the air like spaghetti noodles.

People have invented many different ways for roller coasters to move you around. Some coasters let you ride upside down or zoom backwards. Others take you inside dark tunnels or trick you into thinking you are about to drop straight down into water! It has taken centuries of hard work and imagination to turn roller coasters into the thrilling rides they are today.

The World's Fastest Roller Coasters

Name	Location	Year Opened	Speed in Miles Per Hour
1 Dodonpa	Japan	2001	107 mph
2 Superman: The Escape	California	1997	100 mph
3 Steel Dragon 2000	Japan	2000	95 mph

The roller coasters that are built today are faster than the ones people could build years ago. Their speed is measured in miles per hour (mph), or how many miles the roller coaster could travel in an hour if it continued to move this quickly.

2 From Ice to Steel

The earliest roller coasters were made not of metal, but of ice! In the 1400s, ice sliding was a popular sport in Russia during the long, frosty winters. People rode blocks of wood or ice down ice-covered slopes that stretched from the top of high wooden towers to the ground. Later someone had the idea to add wheels to the sleds so that people could ride them during warmer months, too.

Riders of Russian ice slides sat in the laps of expert guides.

Early French roller coasters were the first roller coasters to run on tracks. In French a roller coaster is called *montagne russe*, which means Russian mountain. Why do you think it is called this?

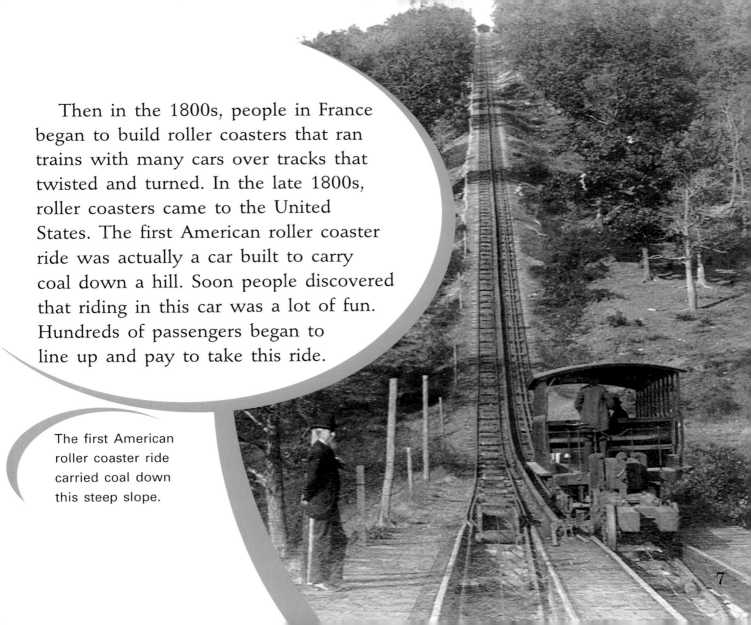

Then in the 1800s, people in France began to build roller coasters that ran trains with many cars over tracks that twisted and turned. In the late 1800s, roller coasters came to the United States. The first American roller coaster ride was actually a car built to carry coal down a hill. Soon people discovered that riding in this car was a lot of fun. Hundreds of passengers began to line up and pay to take this ride.

The first American roller coaster ride carried coal down this steep slope.

7

The first roller coaster built to carry passengers for fun in the United States opened in 1884 in an amusement park in New York. People loved this ride, and soon other wooden roller coasters were built, each more exciting than the last. However, in the 1930s, the Great Depression hit the country. People did not have money to spend on riding roller coasters. Many roller coasters fell apart or were torn down. Then in the 1940s, during World War II, supplies like wood and rubber could not be used to build roller coasters because they were needed for tanks and airplanes instead.

People enjoyed riding this wooden roller coaster in 1915.

After the war ended, people had the time and money to go to amusement parks again. In 1959 a new kind of roller coaster was invented with a track made entirely of steel. Soon steel roller coasters became very popular because they were smoother and quieter to ride than the older wooden roller coasters, and people lined up for these wild rides once again.

Strong, steel roller coasters can whirl people around in many exciting ways.

The History of Roller Coasters (1800–2000)

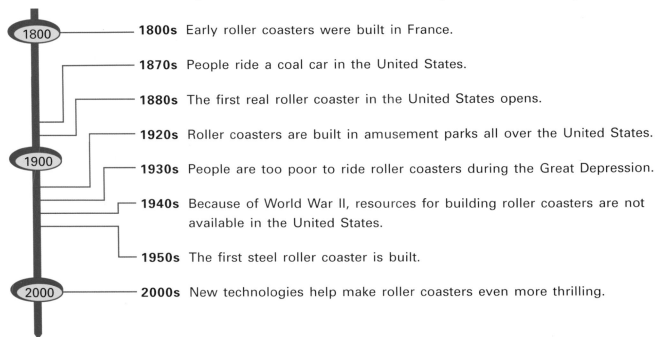

1800 **1800s** Early roller coasters were built in France.

1870s People ride a coal car in the United States.

1880s The first real roller coaster in the United States opens.

1920s Roller coasters are built in amusement parks all over the United States.

1900 **1930s** People are too poor to ride roller coasters during the Great Depression.

1940s Because of World War II, resources for building roller coasters are not available in the United States.

1950s The first steel roller coaster is built.

2000 **2000s** New technologies help make roller coasters even more thrilling.

3 The Science of Wild Rides

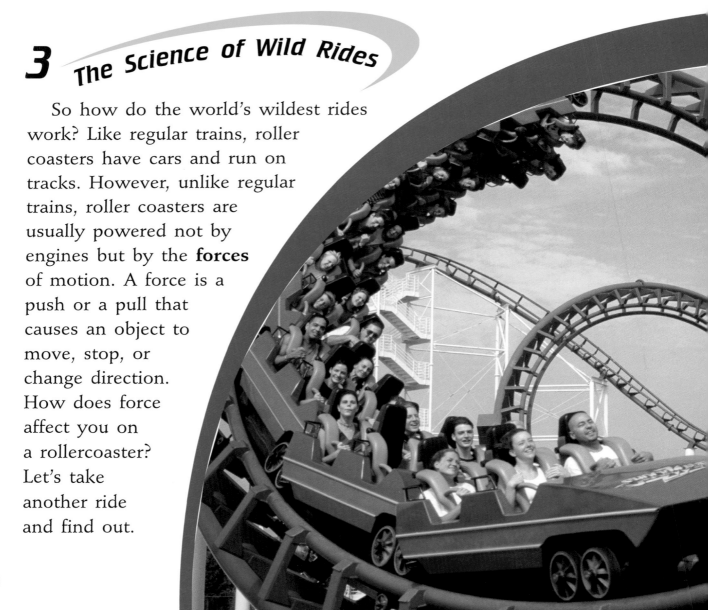

So how do the world's wildest rides work? Like regular trains, roller coasters have cars and run on tracks. However, unlike regular trains, roller coasters are usually powered not by engines but by the **forces** of motion. A force is a push or a pull that causes an object to move, stop, or change direction. How does force affect you on a rollercoaster? Let's take another ride and find out.

After your roller coaster car exits the station, it begins to climb the first hill, called the lift hill. An electric motor pulls the chain underneath the lift hill, and a metal hook under each car catches the chain. As the chain moves, it pulls the hook and drags the car up. At the top of the hill, the hook unfastens. Because everything on Earth is always being pulled toward Earth by the force of **gravity,** the car plunges down the hill toward the ground.

Climbing Up the Lift Hill

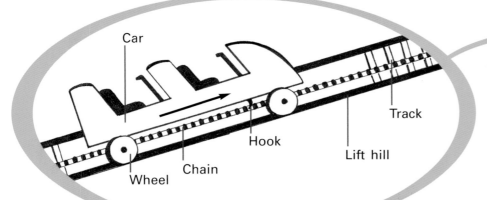

The hook beneath the car catches the chain and pulls the car up the hill. After that, gravity pulls the car down the other side of the hill.

What happens when your roller coaster car suddenly curves to the right? You are thrown against its left side! The inside of the car is bumping into you as it moves to the right because **inertia** keeps your body moving forward in a straight line. Inertia is the force that keeps objects moving the same way they've already been going. Moving objects keep going in the same direction until a new force pushes or pulls on them.

Feeling Inertia

1. You are traveling in a straight line in your roller coaster car.

2. Your roller coaster car takes a sharp turn to the right.

3. Because of inertia, your body keeps moving straight. As the car turns to the right, you bump up against the car's left side!

When your car climbs to the top of a hill and begins suddenly racing down, your body flies out of the seat for a split second—inertia keeps your body traveling upward! But now you notice you are quickly gaining speed on the downhill dive, going faster and faster. This is called **acceleration.** Some coasters can accelerate to speeds of 70 miles per hour—faster than a car zooming down the highway!

Once a coaster starts moving around a track, inertia will keep it moving until an outside force like **friction** stops it. What is friction? Imagine yourself skating down a giant hill. The only way to slow down is to move your foot and tilt the rubber stopper down until it rubs against the ground. This creates friction, a force that causes you to slow down. This is the same force that slows down our roller coaster car.

Friction between the ground and your skate's rubber stopper slows you down to a halt.

Blocks of wood set into the tracks come up and rub against the belly of each coaster car. This creates friction that stops the cars.

As the roller coaster ride ends and you return to the station, the ride operator pulls a **lever** that raises blocks of wood set into the tracks. This wood rubs against pieces of steel on the bottom of your roller coaster car and creates friction. Your car slows down and stops with a jolt. What a ride that was!

4 The Making of an Exciting Adventure

For years people have wanted new rides that are bigger, faster, and more exciting than older ones. Every day people are studying new technologies to create rides that are as exciting (and safe) as possible. They don't want a ride to be boring, but they also don't want to put riders in real danger!

Strong safety bars keep riders in their seats as this roller coaster races through the air.

Planning a Roller Coaster

Roller coasters take their riders on many different adventures, and **designers** are the people who create an exciting theme for each roller coaster. Sometimes a roller coaster invites you to pretend you are on a trip to outer space or racing through the tunnels of a mine. Some roller coasters speed past huge monsters and dinosaurs posed beside the tracks. Designers decorate the tracks, the roller coaster cars, and the area around the roller coaster to help you feel like you really are in these thrilling situations.

The designers of this ride wanted to make riders feel like they've traveled back in time. What objects did they build to do this?

To keep riders safe, **engineers** study how different forces will affect the movement of the roller coaster car. For example, the amount of force needed to move the roller coaster around the track will depend on how heavy the roller coaster is. Engineers also need to think about how heavy the people riding the roller coaster will be. Otherwise, they might not build the right number of hills to give the roller coaster enough speed to make it all the way around the track.

Engineers study all of the forces needed to move a roller coaster's car all the way around the tracks.

Building a Roller Coaster

When the design of the roller coaster is final, construction begins. Usually the parts of the ride are put together in a factory, rather than at the place where the roller coaster will be built. Then the track is shipped in pieces to the amusement park and assembled there. At this point, the roller coaster looks like a giant toy building set.

It takes many different pieces to build a roller coaster.

Safety First!

Once the ride is built, the roller coaster goes through safety tests before you can ride it. The cars of the coaster are loaded with sandbags and sent around the track. The engineers want to make sure that the riders will be safe in the cars and that the cars will not have any problems carrying this weight. Then they try out the ride themselves. Finally once they are sure the ride is completely safe, it is your turn to ride!

Each day before a roller coaster is used, amusement park workers check the ride to be sure it is working safely. They don't want anything to break while people are on it. Therefore, they make sure that everything is safe before they open the park. They do a more detailed safety check every month, and every year they take the entire coaster apart and rebuild it to replace worn-out pieces.

You Must Be This Tall . . .

Most roller coasters say that you have to be a certain height before you can ride them. If you are too small, you might not fit properly into the safety gear in the car as it races around the track.

Daily Safety Routines for Roller Coasters

1. Workers walk down the track of a wooden roller coaster or use binoculars to check the track of steel roller coasters and make sure there are no cracks or loose bolts.

2. Workers check the lift chain and brakes to make sure they are working.

3. Workers look at the roller coaster cars for loose bolts or cracks. They also make sure that the safety bars and other devices are working.

4. Workers send the roller coaster car around the track without riders.

5. Finally workers ride the roller coaster, listening for sounds that could indicate problems.

5 An Engineer Up Close: Jim Seay

So what sort of person designs roller coasters? Jim Seay has won many awards for designing "extreme rides"—rides with the fastest speeds, the greatest number of twists, the steepest drops, and the most excitement. He enjoys his job very much. "You do want people to be scared," Jim says about building roller coasters. "That's the great thing about our business. Our number one goal is to scare people."

Jim has been called his company's Chief Engineer of Fear.

Jim was born in Geneva, Switzerland on April 26, 1960 and moved to Connecticut when he was eight years old. Jim didn't go to many amusement parks as a child, but he does recall one ride on a wooden roller coaster. Of that ride, Jim says, "I just remember it being very thrilling. I think I was scared to death, and I enjoyed it."

Something else had an even bigger effect on Jim, though. When he was nine, people first landed on the moon. This made him very interested in science, including space exploration and especially rockets.

Jim's company designed this thrilling, twisty ride. This type of roller coaster is called a "spaghetti bowl."

23

Along with his love of science, Jim has an interest in speed. He has always liked cars, rocket ships, and motorcycles—all things that people design and redesign to go faster and faster. He also likes adventurous sports, such as racing sailboats, skydiving, and in-line skating. And he loves roller coasters, saying that if a coaster does what it is supposed to do, ". . . you want to ride it over and over. It's a thrill every time."

Jim says he can ride one of his company's coasters over and over and still enjoy it. "Even after 50 times, it's still a thrill," he says.

At first Jim tried to fill his love of speed by studying to be a fighter pilot, but soon he decided he would rather go to college and study engineering. After graduating he helped the army design new ways to guide objects through the air. However, he quit a few years later to take a job where he could mix his love of excitement with his knowledge of technology—creating bigger and better roller coasters.

The roller coasters Jim's company creates can reach top speeds in just a few seconds!

6 New Kinds of Coasters

When amusement parks want to develop wild rides, they hire expert engineers who understand how to move people quickly through the air without hurting them. Because of Jim's experiences in school and with the army, he knows how to make the people riding his roller coasters feel like they are soaring around in a rocket. In fact, he and his company have used technology in their roller coasters that was originally used to blast real rockets off the ground!

Using new technology, Jim's company made this ride that can blast cars to 70 mph in less than four seconds!

On some of the rides Jim has created, you don't begin by being lifted up a big hill. Instead, the coaster shoots straight out the station with an immediate burst of speed. How does this happen?

Strong **electromagnets** line the tracks of these roller coasters. These electromagnets are iron bars made into magnets by passing electricity through wires wrapped around them. The roller coaster cars have metal fins on their bellies, which are attracted to the electromagnets. When a huge amount of electricity runs through the electromagnets surrounding the fins, a magnetic force is created that pushes the cars forward or backward.

Metal fins on the bottom of this coaster glide between pairs of magnets.

27

The Wicked Twister twists people
up into the air and then sends them
spinning back down the track!

The earliest roller coasters could only go up, down, and upside down, but now roller coasters can roll you in sideways circles or swing your legs in mid-air. As people invent new technologies and think of new ideas, roller coasters keep becoming more and more exciting to ride. Each day they get bigger, faster, and more amazing.

Would you like to help build roller coasters in the future? Jim says you should take part in creative activities, study science in school, and learn how to work well in a team. It takes hundreds of people to create each roller coaster. But Jim says, "Any one person can make a difference during that process." That person could be you!

Electric Fun!

The Wicked Twister roller coaster in Ohio uses enough electricity during each ride to power 550 houses!

29

Glossary

acceleration the act of increasing speed

designer a person who decides how a roller coaster should look and move

electromagnet a magnet created by running electricity through special curved wires

engineer a person who uses math and science to create machines like roller coasters

force a push or a pull that causes an object to move, stop, or change direction

friction a force that slows or stops moving objects that are rubbing against something

gravity the force that pulls objects toward the center of Earth

inertia the property of matter that keeps an object moving if it is moving and keeps the object still if it is still

lever a bar that helps lift things

Index